GARDEN CITY PUBLIC LIBRARY
31735 MAPLEWOOD
GARDEN CITY MI 48135
734-793-1830
www.garden-city.lib.mi.us

IMAGES
of America

OLD CHICAGO ROAD

US-12 FROM DETROIT TO CHICAGO

On THE COVER: ROADSIDE ATTRACTION. Pictured are the twin observation towers of the Irish Hills in Onsted, Michigan. Built by two separate owners during the early 1920s, they were once the focus of a feud, earning them the nickname "Spite Towers." (Courtesy of the David V. Tinder Collection of Michigan Photography in the William L. Clements Library, University of Michigan, Ann Arbor.)

IMAGES
of America

OLD CHICAGO ROAD

US-12 FROM DETROIT TO CHICAGO

Jon Milan

ARCADIA
PUBLISHING

Copyright © 2011 by Jon Milan
ISBN 978-1-5316-5169-5

Published by Arcadia Publishing
Charleston, South Carolina

Library of Congress Control Number: 2009943885

For all general information, please contact Arcadia Publishing:
Telephone 843-853-2070
Fax 843-853-0044
E-mail sales@arcadiapublishing.com
For customer service and orders:
Toll-Free 1-888-313-2665

Visit us on the Internet at www.arcadiapublishing.com

CONTENTS

ACKNOWLEDGMENTS

This book could not have been completed without the interest, generosity, and assistance of many individuals. First and foremost, this book could never have been possible without the photographic collection of David V. Tinder. I cannot say enough about Dave's attention, generosity, and kindness. For the most part of an entire year, Dave provided access to his collection, lent his historical expertise and advice, and gave me the benefit of countless hours poring over his collection while sharing historical insights and anecdotes about each and every photograph we encountered. In addition to being an important historian and archivist, Dave is a wonderful human being, and I feel honored to know him and count him among my friends.

In addition to this, I would like to thank my youngest son, Evan C. Milan, for the time and effort spent on my behalf during this long process. Evan rode (and sometimes even drove) along with me countless times between Detroit and Chicago along US-12, taking notes, reading maps, pointing out landmarks, and providing great company.

For spending unselfish hours poring over the manuscript of the book, I would like to thank Gail Offen. A wonderful writer and editor in her own right, Gail's tireless efforts in proofreading, editing, and providing expert advice made the final process much easier and the final product far better than I could have imagined.

Finally, I cannot say enough about the many hours spent by Durwood Coffey, as he tirelessly scanned images and cropped photographs to suit my needs. He is patient, professional, and willing to work all night whenever necessary!

For providing information, research assistance, direction, and encouragement, I would also like to thank Kirt Gross and the Dearborn Historical Museum (Dearborn, Michigan), Richard Story and the Wayne Historical Museum (Wayne, Michigan), Michael Montgomery, Rudy Simons, Charlie Rasch, Howard Rasch, Dorrie Milan, Emily Milan, Benjamin Milan, Romie Minor, Christine Schinker, and Richard and Sharon Sowerby.

Unless otherwise noted, all photographs included in this book are courtesy of the David V. Tinder Collection of Michigan Photography in the William L. Clements Library at the University of Michigan in Ann Arbor, Michigan.

INTRODUCTION

I grew up less than two miles from US-12, and I have never lived more than 10 miles from it. But it has had many names. Where I lived, it was always known as Michigan Avenue, and the US-12 designation was simply something for a map. Yet there were always road signs along the way that clearly displayed the big, bold, black "US-12." Before that, it was US-112. My father always called it the "Old Chicago Road." In more ancient history, it was called the Old Sauk Trail, and it had been walked upon for more than 1,000 years by Native Americans before any European invaders arrived.

Before there was a Detroit or a Chicago, it made sense for a trail to exist between the straits of the Detroit River and the open land around Lake Michigan. As time went on, there were trading posts and military installations in the regions of Detroit and Chicago, and travel between these two points would have increased accordingly.

After the American Revolution and the War of 1812, the territory opened up to American settlement, and the wilderness along the ancient path slowly faded away. We know more about the path during this period than at any time before. Most of the cities and towns along what was once the Old Sauk Trail were settled during this time. During the 1820s and 1830s, the trail became a major stage route, and many people coming from the East settled villages along its path. While they were certainly remote at the time, it is hard to imagine them that way today.

Originally, my plan was to follow the original path (at least as much of it that still remains) and show images of the villages, towns, and cities along the way. The problem is that it is not completely connected the way it once was. From Detroit to Indiana, the road is fairly intact, and little of the route has changed.

In Indiana, the route stays true to the original as far as the city of Gary. After that, the Sauk Trail becomes distorted, re-navigated, and virtually lost, as the route known as US-12 becomes assigned and reassigned to any number of roads and streets that allow it to progress towards Chicago and westward. In addition, urban and industrial development in the area east of Gary and south of Chicago has erased much of the original path.

While the portion of the Sauk Trail that leads westward from the Chicago area is still reasonably intact, the pathway leading to Fort Dearborn (modern-day Chicago) is long gone. Out of respect to history, I have left that area alone rather than attempting any kind of "reconstruction" of this short segment of the route. Though disruption of the original path was more predictable than problematic, other challenges needed to be addressed.

There was the issue of balance. The portion of US-12 that constitutes the Old Sauk Trail from Detroit to Chicago is mostly in the state of Michigan. In fact, from Detroit to Michiana, US-12 covers nearly 250 miles. In Indiana, the route between Michigan City and Chicago's south side is scarcely 60 miles long. And in Chicago, the road (or at least the pathway that would have been the original road) runs a few scant miles.

The positive side of compiling a photograph journal of US-12 in Michigan is that the road leads right through the heart of many of the villages and towns along the way. Unfortunately, this is not the case in Indiana, where the road gently winds along the outskirts of several towns just south of the Indiana Dunes. Throughout the Dunes Region, the roadway is largely picturesque, but outside of the State and National Parks there are virtually no towns directly in its path until it reaches Gary. While Gary affords some landmarks that are noteworthy, it is also the point in which the road loses the true path of the Old Sauk Trail.

Working through these challenges brought clarity to the project, but it also introduced a new dilemma. While the focus would be on the many villages and towns along the way, assembling a collection of historical photographs that covered nearly 300 miles meant coordinating with countless local museums and historical societies. Almost immediately, I found that many of these potential sources were unwilling or unable to lend the needed images to make the project possible.

Fortunately, the project was saved during a visit to one of the many museums along the way. While looking through photographs at the Historical Museum in Dearborn, Michigan, I found myself seated next to Dave Tinder. He was familiar with my first Arcadia publication, *Detroit: Ragtime and the Jazz Age*, and he fully understood the difficulties I had been encountering in assembling the needed photographs for my new project.

I learned that Dave had spent many years assembling the largest collection of vintage Michigan photographs in existence. And, luckily, Dave allowed me full access to any photographs I needed. Soon the David V. Tinder Collection of Michigan Photography would become the centerpiece of my project, and this book is as much a tribute to Dave and his collection as it is to the Old Chicago Road.

I am hopeful that this book provides a worthy introduction to one of America's greatest surviving highways—US-12, the Old Chicago Road, from Detroit to Chicago—and a chance to enjoy the highway in three ways: through information on its origins and history, via a photograph journal of what (and who) was once found along its path, and by way of a visual travelogue of what you might see driving its length today.

Despite a few bumps along the way, it has been a great ride.

One

From Detroit, Westward along the Old Sauk Trail

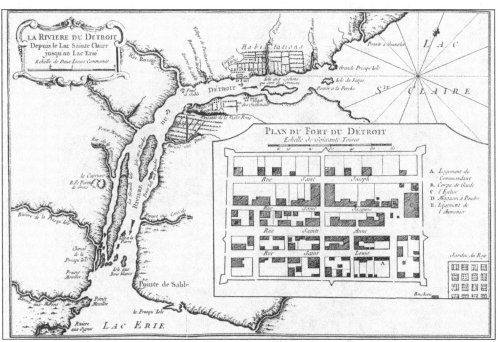

Fort Pontchartrain. Any evidence of Detroit's existence as a French, English, and American fort and trading post was virtually destroyed by the Great Fire of 1805. All that remained was the one thing predating every attempt at Western settlement—the Old Sauk Trail. While the city center was originally established just south of the trail, post-fire plans called for it to be relocated to a spot directly on the path.

THE HUB OF THE WHEEL. The 19th-century stereoscopic view (above) shows Michigan Avenue from its easternmost terminus alongside the base of Detroit's Soldiers and Sailors Monument (1872). The task of creating a new plan for Detroit fell to Augustus Woodward (1774–1827), the first chief justice of the Michigan Territory. Using the street plan of Washington, DC, as a guide, Woodward created a pattern of streets that branched out from Detroit's center. In this configuration, the streets resembled wagon-wheel spokes, ultimately converging at a central hub. While the plan seemed to work in theory, the acute angles at the point of convergence often presented architectural challenges. The 1876 photograph (below) demonstrates just such a challenge, as evidenced by the tapered end of the building that once stood at the convergence of Lafayette and Michigan Avenues.

WESTWARD FROM DETROIT. Generally considered the center of town, Augustus Woodward originally designated the hub of the wheel as Campus Martius. Over the years, it would be known by several names, including Cadillac Square and Kennedy Square, and residents today refer to the place by any one of the three names. Detroit's second city hall, seen above, began operation in 1871 and overlooked Detroit's Campus Martius until it was demolished in 1964. Its north wing abutted with Michigan Avenue. In the stereoscopic view below, two women walk along the portion of Michigan Avenue directly adjacent to the building. Of the structures shown in the stereoscopic views presented here, only the Soldiers and Sailors Monument still stands, having since been incorporated into the park that serves as the modern-day center of Detroit.

TRANSPORTATION AND TRANSITION. Long after the age of the horse and wagon, Woodward's wagon-wheel configuration has remained. And Michigan Avenue, along with the rest of Detroit's major thoroughfares, has adapted accordingly. In the 1917 photograph above, a policeman directs automobile traffic from an elevated traffic tower located at the corner of Michigan and Woodward Avenues. Still, adaptation does not always run smoothly. In the 1943 photograph below, crowds gather along Michigan Avenue, near Second Street, to watch the action (or inaction) after a derailment caused two Detroit Street Railway (DSR) streetcars to suffer a minor collision and become wedged against one another. The incident, no doubt, represented an unavoidable delay for motorists traveling in either direction.

HOT DOG WARS.
The "Coney Island,"
a hot dog lavished in
chili and onions, was
invented in Jackson,
Michigan, in 1914. For
Detroiters, the story
began in 1917 when
"Gust" Keros opened
his American Coney
Island restaurant at
the foot of Michigan
and Lafayette Avenues.
According to legend,
an unresolved business
dispute within the
family resulted in the
establishment of the
adjacent Lafayette
Coney Island. The
competitors have stood
side by side ever since.
(Author's collection.)

CADILLAC HOTEL. Detroit's Cadillac Hotel was built in 1888 and stood at the corner of Michigan Avenue and Washington Boulevard. At the time, it was considered one of Detroit's finest. Among its permanent residents were Dr. James Book, his wife, and three sons—James, Herbert, and Frank. As adults, the brothers entered into partnership, purchased the hotel, and replaced it with the all-new Book-Cadillac Hotel in 1924.

BOOK-CADILLAC HOTEL. Designed by Louis Kamper, the Book-Cadillac Hotel was completed in 1924. Once considered among the finest in America, the grand hotel's successes were later countered by failures and eventual abandonment. Acquired by Westin Hotels in 2006, it underwent a historic $200-million renovation and was officially reopened in 2008. Today, the fully restored gem is considered one of the greatest examples of historic restoration and preservation in the country.

THADDEUS KOSCIUSKO. Just west of Third Street, Michigan Avenue comes under the scrutiny of Gen. Thaddeus Kosciusko (1746–1817), the Polish-Lithuanian hero of the American Revolution. The original statue was cast in 1889, by sculptor Leonard Marconi, for placement on the grounds of Wawel Castle in Poland. In honor of America's bicentennial in 1978, the City of Krakow presented this bronze and granite copy to the City of Detroit. (Author's collection.)

TIGER STADIUM. The corner of Michigan and Trumbull was home to Detroit Tigers baseball for more than 100 years. In 1896, play began on the corner at a stadium known as Bennett Park. It was replaced by Tiger Stadium (shown) in 1912. Originally known as Navin Field, Tiger Stadium was home to, and hosted, many of the greatest players of all time. In 2000, the Tigers moved to Comerica Park.

MICHIGAN CENTRAL STATION. Looming just beyond Roosevelt Park are the ruins of the Michigan Central Railway Station. Built in 1913 as an impressive example of Beaux-Arts architecture, the massive terminal and its 18-story office tower stand empty, windowless, and derelict. Placed in the National Register of Historic Places in 1975, the building has since foundered—a victim of the disintegration of the commuter and passenger railroad industry.

CORKTOWN. Pedestrians stroll the plank sidewalks of Corktown (shown around 1881) near modern-day Rosa Parks Boulevard. Founded in the 1820s by Irish immigrants, Detroit's Corktown is considered the first of many ethnic-based villages and communities established around the perimeter of the city. A second wave of immigration occurred during Ireland's potato famine in the 1840s, forcing Corktown to expand beyond the city limit along Michigan Avenue.

LOOKING BACK. An image from the last years of the era of stereoscopic views shows Michigan Avenue stretching eastward, at a 30-degree angle, from the vicinity of Corktown to the center of Detroit. Dating from the late 1930s, the image shows Detroit at a time when it was one of the world's leading manufacturing centers, the automobile capital of the world, and the fourth largest city in America.

CADILLAC ASSEMBLY PLANT. This c. 1940 photograph shows a truck transporting new Cadillac automobiles from Detroit's Clark Street Cadillac assembly plant. Opened in 1921 as the Cadillac Fleetwood Assembly, the Detroit Cadillac Plant was in operation through 1987 and stood alongside Michigan Avenue between Clark and Scotten Avenues. Today, it is part of the Clark Street Technology Park in the thriving Mexican American community of Detroit known as Mexicantown.

WIDENING MICHIGAN AVENUE. Taken in 1940, this image shows Michigan Avenue undergoing a major road-widening initiative in the shadows of the Cadillac Assembly Plant near the corner of Scotten Avenue. It is obvious that the widening was necessary to accommodate a heavy volume of traffic, as even in the midst of the roadwork, cars, pedestrians, and trolleys continue to move along this busy stretch of Michigan Avenue.

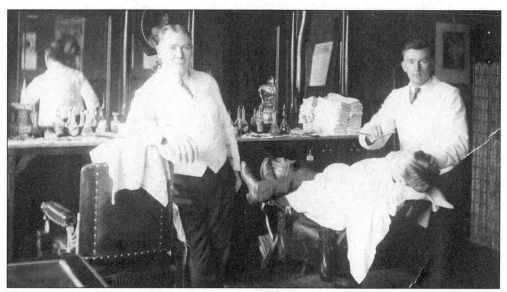

WEST DETROIT. Two barbers stare out from a pre-1910 world in the forgotten village of West Detroit. Founded as Grand Junction in 1859, the area grew up around a railroad station serving six major railway lines and a series of railroad car maintenance and repair facilities for the Michigan Central Railroad. The village was settled by Polish immigrants, chiefly coming from a region known as Lesser (or Malapolska), Poland.

WEST END. Proprietors of the West End Bakery stand with their children in the "lost" village of West End. Detroit was once surrounded by many ethnic villages. West End was settled in 1855 by Ukrainian and Polish immigrants. It stood near the junction of Michigan and Lonyo Avenues and was the last stop on the Westbound Detroit Urban Railway. It was annexed to Detroit in 1906.

GREETINGS FROM DEARBORN. Traveling Westbound from Detroit, the next town along the Old Chicago Road is Dearborn, Michigan. Originally settled in 1795, it was known as Ten Eyck, Bucklin, Dearbornville, and finally Dearborn. The 1910 postcard shown features photographs by J.H. Cave that highlight some of the city's points of interest, including (clockwise from the top left) Michigan Avenue (Wagner Hotel in the center of the image), Dearborn High School, the Arna Mills, and the Rouge River.

DETROIT ARSENAL. In 1833, a federal arsenal was established west of the Rouge River along the Chicago Road. Known as the Detroit Arsenal at Dearbornville, it comprised of 11 buildings, some of which are still extant. In 1875, the US government closed the arsenal, and in 1877 the buildings were sold at auction. The building housing Arna Woolen Mills (shown) originally functioned as the arsenal's armory. It was destroyed by fire in 1910.

THE SUTLER'S SHOP

THE DEARBORN ARSENAL. Several of the buildings comprising the arsenal still stand in the section of town known as West Dearborn. The Sutler's shop, shown above in 1910, originally functioned as a general merchandise store selling clothing, supplies, and tobacco products to soldiers stationed at the arsenal. Today, just a block north of Michigan Avenue, the Sutler's shop still stands, though it has been significantly remodeled to accommodate a medical office. The structures featured in the 1910 postcard below originally functioned as the arsenal's carpenter and smith shops. No longer extant, they are shown during a time when they were occupied by the Detroit-Dearborn Motor Company, one of the many companies that once attempted to capitalize on the burgeoning new automobile industry. Among the Dearbornville Arsenal buildings still extant are the Gun Carriage Shed, the powder magazine (McFadden-Ross House), and the Commandant's Quarters.

DET. DEARBORN MOTOR CO.

THE COMMANDANT'S QUARTERS, 1833. The largest surviving structure from the Dearbornville Arsenal is the Commandant's Quarters. In 1910 (above), it was being used as the Dearborn City Hall. Over the years, it has also functioned as a police station, fire station, library, school facility, meeting hall, and courthouse. Acquired by the Dearborn Historical Commission in 1949, it became the Dearborn Historical Museum in 1950. Today, the building (pictured below) functions as a museum and is part of several historic structures that are operated by the Dearborn Historical Commission as museums and interpretive centers. Over the years, the arsenal gate, a wooden, sentry post station, and a portion of the brick wall that once surrounded the compound have been reconstructed. (Below, author's collection.)

EAST DEARBORN. While the business district that developed around the arsenal is now considered West Dearborn, the city's easternmost business district, which borders Detroit, is considered East Dearborn. In this photograph, heavy pedestrian traffic can be seen around the East Dearborn corner of Michigan Avenue and Schaefer Road. While the photograph dates from the 1930s, the J.M. Schaefer Building (center) continues to present an incredible example of Art Deco architecture today.

ARAB AMERICAN NATIONAL MUSEUM. Over the years, Dearborn's Arabic community has grown and thrived. Today, it is home to one of the largest Arab American communities in the country. It is also home to the Arab American National Museum—the first museum in the world dedicated to Arab American history and culture. Pictured here, the museum is open year-round and is an affiliate of the Smithsonian Institution in Washington, DC. (Author's collection.)

1864 TOLLGATE. For a time during the 19th century, a toll was required for travelling stretches of the Chicago Road. With an increase in migratory traffic, efforts were made to improve the often-muddy road, and portions were graveled, corduroyed, or planked. This monument is located between East and West Dearborn and indicates the site of a tollbooth that once stood along the way. (Author's collection.)

FORD GLASS HOUSE. Within site of the 1864 Chicago Road tollgate—and effecting an amazing then-and-now contrast—is the Glass House, the World Headquarters of the Ford Motor Company. Constructed on property that once belonged to the Henry Ford estate and completed in 1956, the building is considered an important example of an architectural style that is generally referred to as International. (Author's collection.)

West Dearborn. Interurban railway tracks run up the middle of the street in this westward view of Michigan Avenue at Mason Street. The Clara Bryant Library (right) is still in operation as one of Dearborn's public libraries. Beyond the library is the Calvin Theater. Built in 1927, it continued to show movies until it was severely damaged by fire in 1980 and was subsequently demolished.

St Joseph's Retreat. Michigan's first private mental institution stood at the corner of Michigan Avenue and Outer Drive. Founded in 1860 by the Daughters of Charity (St. Vincent de Paul), it began as the Michigan State Retreat. In 1883, it was incorporated as St. Joseph's Retreat, and the building pictured was completed in 1885. Unable to meet expanding demands of modern medical treatment and therapy, it was closed in 1962.

DEARBORN MOTEL, 25925 Michigan Ave., U.S. 112, Inkster (Suburban Detroit) Mich.

DEARBORN IN INKSTER. The Dearborn Motel is actually in Inkster. While Michigan Avenue was being transformed from ancient path to major highway, population shifts were changing the boundaries along its path. By the 1960s, portions of Dearborn Township and Inkster merged, creating the city of Dearborn Heights. While Michigan Avenue crosses only a small stretch of the newly created city, it may have caused confusion for businesses along the way. (Author's collection.)

MOULIN ROUGE. Settled in 1825, Inkster was originally known as Moulin Rouge. It was renamed for local sawmill owner Robert Inkster in 1863. While there was much growth along Michigan Avenue to the east, Inkster remained predominantly rural until the 1920s. This 1914 photograph shows horse-drawn wagons flanking the entranceway to the Brown Bros. General Store, which was one of the few businesses in Inkster at the time.

INKSTER, MICHIGAN, 1919. An automobile and a horse-drawn wagon stand at opposite sides of Michigan Avenue in Inkster in 1919. It is difficult to imagine this rural setting could be found just seven miles from one of the largest cities in America. Connected by the interurban track running up the middle of the street, this scene was merely minutes away from a world of theaters, jazz, nightclubs, and speakeasies.

ROADSIDE AMERICA. By the 1950s, Inkster had come into the modern age, and that same stretch of Michigan Avenue was suddenly lined with tourist cabins, motels, and motor lodges. Before the era of superhighways, Michigan Avenue was the preferred route to Detroit, Chicago, and all points west. With the added attraction of Greenfield Village and the Henry Ford Museum just three miles away, motels like the Del Rio (shown) thrived. (Author's collection.)

LOOKING ACROSS THE LAKE EL OISE Mich

ELOISE. In 1839, the County Poorhouse in Detroit was relocated to a remote place in the wilderness, where the Chicago Road crosses the Merriman Road. Originally the site of a stagecoach stop known as the Black Horse Tavern, the place soon became a convenient repository for alcoholics, drug addicts, and the mentally ill. Eventually, it would encompass more than 75 buildings, over 902 acres, and come to be known as Eloise. By the time the 1917 photograph above was taken, the grounds included a working farm, manufacturing facilities, and a train station on the Detroit Urban Railway, shown below. Renamed Eloise in 1894 for the daughter of a board executive, the expansive complex was eventually divided to accommodate its role as a "hospital for the insane" while also offering services as an infirmary for the sick and elderly.

CITY OF ELOISE. By the 20th century, Eloise literally became a city unto itself. It had a post office, fire department, police department, library, and even a theater, as well as a laundry, bakery, and general store (pictured). At times, the inmate and employee population exceeded 10,000, and as many as 20 percent of the employees lived on the grounds.

POWERHOUSE. Eloise generated much of its own electricity. The power plant (shown) was located near the center of the complex. In 1981, given operating expenses and changes in psychiatric care, Eloise was closed. Since then, most of the land has been sold and the buildings demolished. The surviving Kay Beard Building now functions as a county office and houses a small, public museum dedicated to the history of Eloise.

I Want You to See Wayne. This postcard from about 1910, complete with pre-printed artwork, was one of several available to municipalities across the country. Often referred to as a generic card, the name of the location was merely overprinted according to the buyer's purchase order. In this case, the automobile motif is appropriate. Over the years, Wayne hosted several automotive concerns, including Harroun, Graham-Paige, and a Ford production facility. (Author's collection.)

Brownie's Diner. This iconic, neon diner sign still beckons travelers along US-12 to Brownie's, an old Wayne favorite and survivor in the fading tradition of the small-town eatery. Founded in 1939 by Melvin Brown, Brownie's has been owned and operated by Frances Howard since 1972, and she continues to offer its traditional, home-style fare and service in an age of fast-food giants and nationwide franchises. (Author's collection.)

JOHNSON'S TAVERN. Pictured above, Wayne began when George Johnson built a tavern on this site in 1824. He sold out to Stephen G. Simmons a year later. Here, in 1830, Simmons murdered his wife in a drunken rage and was subsequently tried and hanged—the last man executed under the death penalty in Michigan. Only a few buildings in the photograph still stand along the north side of Michigan Avenue. They are nearly all that remain of Wayne's historic business district, which was demolished in a controversial—and nearly disastrous—urban renewal program. The Commercial Hotel is seen below in a 1904 postcard. Constructed in 1868, the building has somehow managed to survive. For reasons lost to time, the sender of this postcard included a cryptic and ominous note written in reverse (to be read in a mirror): "Not dead but forgotten." (Below, author's collection.)

WAYNE DUR STATION. The Detroit Urban Railway's Wayne depot stood on the southeast corner of Michigan Avenue and Wayne Road. At one time, it was the most efficient means of travel throughout the Detroit area, allowing passengers travel to Ypsilanti, Plymouth, Northville, and on into Detroit. The system ran from the 1890s through the 1920s before the automotive industry and its political influences put the railway out of business.

HARROUN. Still standing along US-12 (although altered) is the Harroun manufacturing plant. After winning the first Indianapolis 500, Ray Harroun decided to become an "auto baron." Naming the newly designed car after himself, Harroun began production in 1916, but not for long. Halted and hampered by World War I, an armament commission, and then the postwar depression, Harroun was quickly out of business. The plant (as pictured) later became a Graham-Paige body plant.

CHICAGO ROAD TOLLHOUSE. Very few images exist of the tollhouses that once stood along the Old Chicago Road. This faded image was taken in the mid-19th century just west of Wayne near a no-longer-extant junction with Cogswell Road. Not far from this site, a portion of the Rouge River was dammed to create Carpenters Lake, a popular tourist destination that remained into the 1920s. (Courtesy of the Wayne Historical Museum.)

EILA'S. West of Wayne, the landscape is more sparsely populated, still showing remnants of an agricultural past. According to this postcard, Eila's Restaurant specialized in steaks, fried chicken, and hamburger deluxes. This diner has had many names over the years and is still an operating business today. While this region is now considered Canton, in years past it shared mailing addresses with Belleville, Van Buren Township, and Sheldon Corners. (Author's collection.)

SHELDON CORNERS. Westward towards Sheldon and Canton Center Roads, Michigan Avenue passes through the lost village of Sheldon Corners. The image above shows the regional post office alongside the village grocery store. At one time, the two businesses were competitors, standing at opposite sides of the street. The 1911 photograph was taken after the building housing the grocery store was relocated. The Sheldon Creamery, seen below, is presented in another image dating from 1911. While these businesses no longer exist, some buildings dating from the early years of Sheldon Corners still stand. Among them are the Sheldon Schoolhouse (1890) and the Sheldon Inn (1825), which once functioned as a stagecoach stop along the Chicago Road (now a private home). Stein's Flowers and Greenhouses is a more recent vintage business of the region (1950), continuing today as Keller and Stein.

SHELDON WAYNE PARK LUNCH. During the early years of the 20th century, the area surrounding Sheldon Corners became a popular getaway for Detroiters hoping to escape the daily grind of urban life. In those days, Sheldon Corners was "out in the country," and businesses like the Sheldon Wayne Park Lunch (above) once thrived, catering to the needs of the new breed of travelers along the highway.

SHARR MOTEL. Michigan Avenue was US-112 when the Sharr Motel stood near Sheldon Corners. Targeting modern, postwar travelers, the Sharr offered rooms with radios and black-and-white televisions and was a familiar site for many years. With an accelerated increase in commercial, industrial, and residential development along this stretch, most of the old remnants of roadside America, including the Sharr, have long since disappeared. (Author's collection.)

THE DENTON SCHOOL

VILLAGE OF DENTON. For tracking towns along Old Chicago Road, the village of Denton almost does not count. From Michigan Avenue, the only parts visible are a farmhouse and barn, a small church, a few smaller houses, and the Denton Cemetery. Most of Denton was located along the Denton Road, on the section running south between Michigan Avenue and the Michigan Central Railroad tracks. Unfortunately, there is almost nothing left of the old village—at least, nothing that would identify it once as being a central business district. Named for Samuel T. Denton, the village grew up around a Michigan Central Railroad station, dating from 1864, and the South Plymouth Post office, which operated in the village until 1933. Neither the Denton School (above) nor the post office (below, in a 1910 postal card photograph) are still extant.

POST OFFICE - DENTON MICH

Kaiser-Frazer Corp. Plant, WILLOW RUN, MICH.

WILLOW RUN. In the late 1930s, Henry Ford converted property near Ypsilanti, Michigan, into a summer camp. Named Willow Run, it briefly functioned as a working farm for underprivileged boys, but that did not last long. With war raging in Europe, the government was offering lucrative contracts to companies willing to manufacture arms for its European allies. Seeing an enormous profit opportunity, Ford abandoned the camp and in 1941 built the B-24 Liberator Bomber Plant. Designed by Albert Kahn, the 3.5-million-square-foot facility was the largest ever constructed and featured an unusual *L*-shaped turn, which enabled Ford to avoid the higher taxes levied by the adjacent county. After the United States entered the war, production increased steadily, and the plant turned out 8,685 B-24 bombers before closing in 1945. Afterwards, the facility became an assembly plant for Kaiser-Frazer Automotive.

KAISER

One Every Minute Is Not Enough!

FRAZER

Production scheduled at Willow Run now exceeds a car every minute. But even 12,000 KAISERS and FRAZERS a month are nowhere near enough! For our many thousands of owners are our best salesmen. They have discovered something *totally new*—in *beauty*, in *performance*, and, above all, in *ride!* They tell their friends—their friends take a ride—and order a KAISER or a FRAZER. If *you* drove even five miles in one of these 100% postwar automobiles, you would want one, too. Why not try it? *Wherever you are*, there is a Kaiser-Frazer dealer near you.

KAISER-FRAZER CORPORATION • WILLOW RUN, MICHIGAN

KAISER-FRAZER. This 1947 advertisement appeared in the *Saturday Evening Post* during a short-lived period of success and prosperity for the Kaiser-Frazier Corporation. Founded in 1945 through a partnership between Joseph W. Frazier and Henry J. Kaiser, the company was able to lease the recently vacated Willow Run B-24 Liberator Bomber Plant for use as its production facility. Drawing on the vast pool of available labor left over from production during the war years—as well as the availability of servicemen returning from the war looking for work—the newly formed automotive concern was able to use the immense facility to their full advantage. In fact, by the time this advertisement ran, Kaiser-Frazer was able to boast of production levels that exceeded one vehicle per minute, totaling 12,000 every month. The success of Kaiser-Frazer was short-lived, however, and production at the Willow Run facility ended in 1953. Shortly thereafter, the Willow Run plant was sold to the General Motors Corporation. (Author's collection.)

VIEWS OF YPSILANTI. Following Michigan Avenue along its westward path from Detroit to Chicago, Ypsilanti is the first city encountered in Washtenaw County, which was created in 1827. Established in 1825, Ypsilanti eventually absorbed the village of Woodruff's Grove, established in 1823, and sits along the Chicago Road where it crosses the Huron River. The Michigan State Normal College was established here in 1849. It was the first teachers college to be established outside of the original 13 colonies, and in later years it became Eastern Michigan University. During the 19th century, Ypsilanti was also known for its mineral baths and mineral salts and was a popular destination for individuals seeking the "curative" powers of these natural wonders. This 1908 postcard features several of the buildings and sites that existed throughout the city at the time, many of which still stand. Ypsilanti is rich in local history and still maintains many of its historic structures. Among its most famous residents were inventor Elijah McCoy (1844–1929) and automobile entrepreneur Preston Tucker (1903–1956). (Author's collection.)

BILL'S HOT DOGS. The tiny, bright yellow shack standing on the eastern end of Ypsilanti has been a local favorite for more than 60 years. Known for its three-item menu, Bill's has delighted patrons since 1950 with its own unique variety of hot dogs slathered in chili, potato chips, and root beer. In a daring move, the menu recently expanded to include more than one flavor of soft drink. (Author's collection.)

ROY'S SQUEEZE INN. Ypsilanti hosts a fair share of vintage drive-ins left over from the golden age of roadside America. Directly across from Bill's, Roy's Squeeze Inn has offered both in-car and counter service since 1959. Serving up a wide variety of award-winning drive-in favorites, Roy's maintains its original look and feel. It was even used for scenes in the 2010 motion picture *Conviction*. (Author's collection.)

CONGRESS STREET BRIDGE. Michigan Avenue is known by many names as it meanders between Detroit and Chicago. In Ypsilanti, it was known as Congress Street during the 19th century. In this photograph, factories and smokestacks beyond the Congress Street Bridge reveal the strong industrial foundations of the city. At the time, Ypsilanti flourished with paper mills, woolen mills, breweries, and manufacturing concerns of national renown.

THE YPSI-ANN. While Michigan's network of interurban railroads became a popular and fast mode of travel during the late 19th and early 20th centuries, the line between Ypsilanti and Ann Arbor was the first in the state. Known locally as the Ypsi-Ann, the interurban line (shown) was an immediate success, particularly with students traveling between the University of Michigan, in Ann Arbor, and Ypsilanti's State Normal College.

HAAB'S. An inside glimpse of travel along the Old Chicago Road is still available at Haab's Restaurant in Ypsilanti. Founded in 1934—just after Prohibition—by brothers Otto and Oscar Haab, the building has continuously housed a restaurant and bar (when possible) since 1850. Still extant are the original tin ceilings, the great mahogany bar, and the wall that once divided the ladies' and men's sections of the saloon. (Author's collection.)

CLEARY BUSINESS COLLEGE. Founded as the Cleary School of Penmanship in 1883, Cleary Business College moved into the building at the corner of Michigan Avenue and Adams Street (shown) in 1888. Though extensively damaged in Ypsilanti's 1893 tornado, the school continued to occupy the site for many years. Among its most famous students is illustrator Winsor McCay. While still in operation, the school is no longer located on Michigan Avenue.

YPSILANTI BANK. Built in 1887, the Ypsilanti Savings Bank building still stands at Michigan Avenue and Huron Street. It has been Ypsilanti's city hall since 1977. Unfortunately, the structure no longer has its distinctive gabled roof, which was replaced in a much earlier alteration. In recent years, Ypsilanti has taken full advantage of its vintage architecture, and restoration efforts continue throughout its many historic districts.

SCHMIDT'S. Heading west from Ypsilanti, the road winds through Pittsfield Township and soon passes a familiar local landmark: the statuary, barn, silo, and main buildings of Schmidt's Antiques. Founded in 1911, the company has been family owned for four generations and has occupied the current site for more than 70 years. Specializing in European antiques, Schmidt's is known throughout the region for its large, fascinating showrooms and regularly scheduled auctions. (Author's collection.)

A Trip to Saline, Michigan. A souvenir postcard depicts early-20th-century scenes from the city of Saline, Michigan, predominantly a farming community at the time. The featured photographs include the local baseball team, churches, the railroad depot, and the city's largest estate. Founded in 1832, the city stands just west of the Saline River, and both were named for the abundant salt springs found in the area.

Rentschler Farm. Just east of Saline, the road passes the Rentschler Farm. Established in 1901, the farm was owned and operated by four generations of the Rentschler family before Saline purchased it in 1998. Through the ongoing efforts of the Saline Historical Society and its volunteers, the farmhouse and its 11 outbuildings now function as a public museum, depicting farm life during the early 20th century. (Author's collection.)

MICH. AVE. RESIDENTIAL VIEW
SALINE MICH.

SALINE'S TREE-LINED AVENUE AND THE DAVENPORT-CURTISS HOUSE. The approach to downtown Saline along Michigan Avenue still looks somewhat the same as it did in the 1928 photograph above. Much of it is still lined with trees, and many of the old clapboard frame houses still stand. Still waiting at the end of the eastbound approach is the immense, awe-striking home and grounds of the Davenport-Curtiss House, seen at left. Originally the home of William H. Davenport (1826–1909), the house was built in 1875 and designed in the Second Empire style by Detroit architect William Scott, who also designed the Wayne County Courthouse and Ann Arbor Firehouse. Davenport was a successful Saline businessman who founded and served as president of a bank that eventually became the Citizens' Bank of Saline. After his death, the home belonged to Carl Curtiss (1883–1967), who also served as president of the bank. (At left, author's collection.)

SALINE'S HISTORIC DOWNTOWN DISTRICT. An interurban is pictured above in mid-turn in the middle of Chicago Street as it works its way through downtown Saline. The eastbound view shown in the 1910 photograph is, surprisingly, not too different from the view afforded to pedestrians walking the streets of Saline today. The same can be said of the vintage photograph below, which offers a westbound view that includes the Saline Savings Bank and Burkhart's General Store. In both photographs, many of the buildings shown are still in existence, and in recent years the city of Saline has made great efforts to ensure their restoration and preservation.

SALINE MILL AND DAM. Standing on the south side of Michigan Avenue, just west of town, is a sight that should be familiar to any local resident of the past 165 years. Though it has been expanded by additions, altered, and more than once restored, the site of the Schuyler Flour Mill has dominated Saline's western horizon since 1845. The mill saw new life in 1935, when it was purchased by Henry Ford as part of a program that briefly employed farms and rural mills in processing soybeans for industrial use. Both photographs show the mill and dam while still in use by the Ford Motor Company. Years later, the facility was purchased by the Weller family and again restored. Since then, it has been a café, an antiques store, and ultimately a popular banquet facility.

MASTODON TRACKS. In 1992, Harry Brennan was digging a pond on his land, located west of Saline along US-12, when he discovered something that looked like the footprints of a very large creature. Assuming they were of archeological importance, he contacted the University of Michigan. After a thorough examination of the site, paleontologist Daniel Fischer informed Brennan that his assumption was correct. He had inadvertently unearthed "the largest and most complete mastodon trackway ever found." Consisting of 30 prints, some measuring as much as 20 inches across, Fischer concluded that the tracks had been left by a male that stood nine feet tall and weighed about six tons. The trackway remains in a protected area designated as the Brennan Site. Too fragile to move, the 10,000-year-old trackway was reproduced in an immense 40-foot plastic mold and is now on display at the Ruthven Exhibit Museum at the University of Michigan. (Author's collection.)

OLD STAGE HOUSE
CLINTON, MICH

CLINTON. Westbound beyond Saline, the road reveals a glimpse of its old self; towns appear sparsely, and rolling farms and deep woods spread across the Mississippian topography. Built in 1830, the Stage House (shown) was once the Clinton Inn, a stage stop along the trail. All but abandoned in 1925, it was purchased by Henry Ford and moved to Dearborn, where it was restored. Today, it is the Eagle Tavern of Greenfield Village.

CLINTON INN AND THE LSMSR. The tower of the second Clinton Inn (above, right) is still a familiar landmark for travelers along the Chicago Road. Located at the eastern end of Clinton, the historic hotel was built by Alonzo Clark in 1901. Still in business, today the restored inn offers year-round dining and lodging. The village of Clinton was incorporated in 1838 but was a familiar stop along the stage route long before. Named for DeWitt Clinton, the New York governor known as the "Father of the Erie Canal," the village was also a rail stop (below) along the Lake Shore & Michigan Southern Railway. While the original railroad concern no longer exists, the station now functions as an rail station museum, operated by the Southern Michigan Railroad Society. Through its efforts, the once-abandoned tracks are now used for excursions between Clinton and Tecumseh.

MAIN STREET AND THE CLINTON WOOLEN MILLS. A cyclist rides amid horse-drawn wagons (above), but there is not a single automobile in sight in this eastbound, early-20th-century view of Michigan Avenue in Clinton, Michigan. A lone streetlamp is suspended across the road in the foreground, and the tower of the Clinton Inn is clearly visible in the left background. While the scene has greatly changed over the years, many of the buildings pictured still stand. The Clinton Woolen Mills (below in 1886) was once the chief employer in Clinton. Founded in 1866, the original mill was destroyed by fire and replaced by the mill shown. By the early 20th century, the mill became a primary source of wool fabric for automobile upholstery. It closed in 1957, around the same time that the automotive industry began using synthetic fabrics.

Two

INTO THE INTERIOR
THE IRISH HILLS AND BEYOND

INTO THE HILLS. The Woolen Mill is shown in 1954, when Clinton was known as the Woolen Mill Town. Clinton is part of the Irish Hills region, and beyond town the road begins twisting and turning between dark, shadowy wooded hills. Known to be rife with highwaymen and "renegade Indians," the region was feared by stagecoach travelers. They could not have imagined what they would have encountered here less than a century later. (Author's collection.)

TOURIST TRAIL. By the 1920s, the Irish Hills was in the throes of a tourism gold rush. And as automobile travel along the Old Chicago Road became common, the Irish Hills suddenly transformed into a tourist wonderland. The beautiful rolling landscape and the abundant lakes of the region made the Irish Hills a popular vacation destination and a frequent stop along the roadway for travelers. From the early 1920s through the late 1960s, new tourist attractions seemed to sprout up everywhere along the route. Standing at left without a friend in the world in the abandoned parking lot of the Stagecoach Stop, a once-popular Wild West theme park, Paul Bunyan leers at travelers from behind his mighty ax. Below, a vacationer from the early 1960s seems delighted to defy the laws of gravity during a stop at Mystery Hill. (Both author's collection.)

DINO HAZARD. Above, a ferocious, yet completely unidentifiable species of dinosaur stares out at US-12 from the ruins of Prehistoric Forest. Built along the strip in the early 1960s, the amusement park featured guided tram rides through re-created prehistoric landscapes that included mountains, forests, tar pits, dinosaurs, mastodons, and cavemen constructed of plaster, wire, concrete, and whatever other materials were available—all with little or no regard for historical accuracy. The once-popular theme park was in business for nearly 40 years before time, and the nearby superhighway, forced it to go the "way of the dinosaur." Below, a stylized brontosaurus sculpture rests its decaying head on the pole that used to be a giant palm tree. (Both author's collection.)

THE IRISH HILLS OBSERVATORY
SOUTHERN MICHIGAN

THE TWO TOWERS. In 1924, the Michigan Observatory Company (MOC) decided to cash in on the booming tourist trade in the Irish Hills by building an observation tower. Their desired location was atop Brighton Hill, occupying the highest elevation in the area and conveniently standing alongside US-12. Unfortunately, ownership of the hill was divided at the top between land purchased by the MOC and acreage owned neighbor Edward Kelley, who was bitterly opposed to the plan. After exhausting every avenue to stop the tower from materializing, Kelly vented his anger in a completely unexpected way. He built his own tower just over the property line directly adjacent to the MOC tower. The 1924 photograph above is a view of the MOC tower when it was the only one occupying Brighton Hill. Below, tourists enjoy the view from the observation deck.

IRIS HILLS
MICH 22

IN SPITE OF IT ALL. When the MOC tower was completed, it stood 50 feet tall. Locals said Kelly built his tower 10 feet taller out of spite. The towers soon earned the nickname "Spite Towers" when the MOC countered Kelley by adding 14 feet to their own tower, making it 64 feet tall. Kelley added the additional four feet to equal the MOC tower's height, but he was warned that any further additions would result in the MOC building a giant steel tower that he could never afford to compete with; at that point, the height contest ended. But the competition for customers continued for many years until both towers were bought by a single owner. In the photograph above, a tour bus approaches the twin towers; the postcard below shows the hotel that stood next to the towers for many years.

55

ST. JOSEPH'S CHURCH AND SHRINE. As the Chicago Road meanders westward from Onsted through Brooklyn, it passes the grounds of the historic St. Joseph's Wayside Church and Shrine. Built by Irish immigrants as a missionary church in 1854, the church, seen at left, served the region for many years. In 1928, a shrine was added to the site, and during the Great Depression Mexican artisans were commissioned to create fascinating walkways and sculptures depicting biblical scenes along the steep bank overlooking Iron Lake. Specializing in an unusual form of wet cement sculpture, the Mexican artisans were once highly active in the Irish Hills region, and examples of their work include sculpted objects that have the actual look and feel of trees and wood. The postcard below shows the entrance to St. Joseph's Shrine and the walkway leading to the sculptures along Iron Lake. (Below, author's collection.)

Entrance to Way of the Cross Shrine, St. Joseph's Church

On U. S. 112, Irish Hills, Michigan

WALKER TAVERN. Cambridge Junction is located along the Old Chicago Road, where it crosses La Plaisance Road (later known as the Monroe Pike). The structure, now known as the Walker Tavern, was built in 1836 on a hill alongside the crossroads by Calvin Snell. The structure and adjoining land was purchased by Sylvester Walker and his wife, Lucy, in 1843. Migrating from Cooperstown, New York, where they had been innkeepers, the Walkers aspired to create a similar business for travelers in the Michigan Territory. Establishing the Snell property as the Walker Tavern, they greatly expanded the site to better provide food, lodging, and livery accommodations for travelers along the route. The photograph above shows the Walker Tavern on the hill overlooking US-12. The image below presents a front view of the historic structure prior to restoration.

ORIGINAL AND BRICK WALKER TAVERNS. To accommodate an increasing flow of traffic along the Chicago Road, in 1853 Walker built a larger, three-story brick structure directly across the road. The photograph above shows the original Walker Tavern in the background (right) and the 1853 brick structure in the foreground. In time, the larger brick structure became known as the Brick Walker Tavern. Among the many travelers who once stayed at the historic taverns are author James Fenimore Cooper (1789–1851) and American statesman Daniel Webster (1782–1852). In addition to his work as an innkeeper, Walker was appointed postmaster for the area in 1840 and later became a member of the Michigan State Legislature. The photograph below shows the Brick Walker Tavern during a Fourth of July celebration in the early years of the 20th century.

HISTORIC WALKER TAVERN. In 1865, shortly after the death of Sylvester Walker, the taverns and adjoining land were purchased by Francis Dewey, a former stagecoach driver. Dewey was actively involved in preserving and writing about local history, and he was keenly aware of the tavern's historical significance. In 1922, the site was purchased by Frederick Hewitt, who added to the tourist-friendly landscape of the Irish Hills region by converting the site into a museum and interpretive center. In the postcard photograph at right, tour guides in the early 1920s await visitors while dressed in period costumes dating from the tavern's vintage past. Below, a souvenir postcard shows the tavern's restored taproom. Today, the Walker Tavern Complex is a Michigan State Historic Park. Though the Brick Walker Tavern still stands, it is not currently a part of the historic complex.

THE DAYS OF WINE AND RACING. Just beyond the Walker Taverns, as the road meanders through the outskirts of Brooklyn, the expansive grounds and grandstands of the Michigan International Speedway (MIS) come into view (above). Opened in 1968, the MIS now hosts some of the most notable annual races of the National Association for Stock Car Auto Racing (NASCAR). The Irish Hills area is on the eastern fringe of Michigan's wine-producing region, and perhaps the first evidence of this is the Cherry Creek Winery. Located in the restored Woodstock No. 2 Schoolhouse (below), which was originally built in 1860, the winery offers visitors an opportunity to sample many of its unique products, including a wide variety of wines, cherry preserves, artisan olive oil, and balsamic vinegar. Originally known as Woodstock when settled in 1838, the region was renamed Cement City in 1900. (Both author's collection.)

SOMERSET. When the Chicago Road crosses US-127, it passes westbound into Somerset Township. Settled in the 1830s, the region began with the establishment of two separate villages, Somerset and Somerset Centre (later Center). As with many of the villages in the Irish Hills, the Somerset region was originally settled by families from western New York, and Somerset (in all its configurations) is named for a city in New York's Niagara County. While the two Somerset villages still stand along the route, many of the buildings depicted here have disappeared. The undated photograph above shows the "sprawling" Somerset Centre business district. Below, the Somerset Center School appears in a 1907 photograph taken during a school reunion.

SOMERSET TOWNSHIP VILLAGES. Records indicate that Somerset Centre (Center) was named for its location at the center of Somerset Township. In any case, it was the larger of the two unincorporated Somerset villages. The township also includes the smaller villages of Bakers and Jerome. During the early years of the 20th century, Somerset Centre had its own train station, pictured above, and was the location of the township post office. The photograph below shows a more detailed view of Somerset Centre's business district. The photograph card, postmarked 1913, provides greater detail of the scene shown on the previous page.

McCOURTIE PARK. Perhaps the most fascinating attraction in Michigan's Somerset Township is McCourtie Park. Situated along Michigan Avenue, just west of Jackson Road, the park somehow runs the gamut from a pristine, natural setting to bizarre and even creepy. Developed in the early 1920s by local cement baron H.L. McCourtie, the park, which includes a stream and two spring-fed ponds, was once part of the grounds of the McCourtie estate. Enlisting the talents of local Mexican cement artisans George Cardosa and Ralph Cardona, McCourtie had the grounds decorated with 17 cement bridges made to resemble logs and freshly hewn lumber. He also had them create cement trees that once functioned as chimneys. (Both author's collection.)

BIRDHOUSES AND THE WOMAN IN BLUE. After the death of H.L. McCourtie in 1933, the estate and grounds passed through many hands before ultimately becoming a public park in 1987. Along with the unusual bridges, the park also has an unusual variety of birdhouses, making it a popular place for bird-watching. While the McCourtie home is no longer extant, a section of McCourtie's "hidden" rathskeller still stands— camouflaged as part of a hill. Once rumored to be a private distillery used by bootleggers, the semi-underground building has since been subdivided into separate compartments and garages. Some say that a mysterious woman in blue is often seen strolling along this area, disappearing when anyone comes close enough to investigate. (Both author's collection.)

Lake Shore Station, Moscow, Mich.

Your Friends in

Moscow

Would Like a Glimpse of You

MOSCOW ON THE AVENUE. According to the early-20th-century postcard at right, "Your Friends in Moscow Would Like a Glimpse of You"—although even if this souvenir card had been the most popular in town, it is doubtful that the sum total of everyone's friends in Moscow managed to purchase anywhere near 100 of these generic cards. The small inset photograph in the card shows Moscow's Lake Shore Station. A tiny village along Michigan Avenue, Moscow was settled in 1831 and named by Alonzo Kies, who migrated from Moscow, New York. It is presumed that New York's Moscow was named after the one in Russia. The photograph below shows the bustling Michigan "metropolis" around 1910.

MOSCOW TAVERN AND MOSCOW PLAINS CHURCH. While many structures were demolished long ago, some of Moscow's original buildings still stand along the path of US-12. The Old Moscow Plains Church, shown above, and its still-active cemetery continue to be familiar sites to passersby along Michigan Avenue. Pictured below, the Moscow Tavern was one of the earliest stagecoach stops along the Old Chicago Road. For many years during the 20th century, it functioned as an antiques store, and people came to look for the familiar site of Nellie the mannequin standing out near the front door. Unfortunately, years of neglect took a heavy toll on the structure, which was built around 1830, and it was ultimately demolished.

BIG OAK CAMP AND MILNES. Pictured above in 1933 is one of the many tourist camps that appeared along Michigan Avenue during the 1920s and 1930s, when the road was known as US-112. The Big Oak Camp is fronted by a converted frame house serving as a Standard service station and lunch counter. The message on back of this card reads, "Hello, Gang! Going like Hell—stopped here for lunch. Walter and mother were starved! Getting Hot!" Just down the road from Moscow was the tiny village of Milnes. The old stone schoolhouse, seen below, still stands, though most of the village has long disappeared. What little remains stands where Milnes Road meets Michigan Avenue on an angle from the southwest.

DOWNTOWN MILNES. With a westward view along Michigan Avenue, the postal-card photograph above shows the Milnes General Store, fronted by a line of locals with their horse-drawn vehicles, on a wintery day about 100 years ago. The Milnes School, which now functions as a private business, can be seen in the background. The photograph below was taken at a point between the store and the school and provides a view of Michigan Avenue looking eastward from the village of Milnes. A lone automobile and a horse-drawn carriage sit along the right side of the road. The small slant-roofed structure in front of the Milnes store sports a hand-painted sign that simply reads, "Gasoline."

Air View - Jonesville Mich.

534

JONESVILLE. The village of Jonesville, Michigan, and a portion of US-12 are seen in the aerial photograph above. The c. 1940 image reveals Jonesville to be one of the larger small towns along the Old Sauk Trail, at least in contrast to the small villages throughout the Irish Hills region. Originally settled in 1831 by Benaiah Jones, of Painesville, Ohio, the village was named in his honor and incorporated in 1855. Below, an undated photograph from the early 20th century shows Jonesville's Main Street (actually Michigan Avenue). Later known as Chicago Street, the road is pictured, in a westbound view from Evans Street, during some sort of unidentified street fair or local festival.

MAIN ST. WEST FROM EVANS JONESVILLE, MICH

CHICAGO STREET, JONESVILLE, MICHIGAN. Jonesville appears to be a busy place in the photograph above, captured during the mid-1920s. Michigan Avenue is shown, looking eastbound, after the street name had changed from Main to Chicago Street. The photograph below depicts a late-1920s westbound view of Chicago Street from the corner of Evans Street. In the foreground at left is the Hi-Speed Gas station, once a major brand of gasoline and a familiar sight along the highway. While most of the historic structures that line Jonesville's main business district are still standing, a portion of the block on the northwest end of Michigan Avenue suffered considerable damage in a 2009 fire.

CHICAGO ST. LOOKING WEST—
ALLEN, MICH. 364-A1.

ALLEN. With a population totaling 250, Allen, Michigan, might be considered a very small town—a don't-blink-or-you'll-miss-it kind of place. But, as many people throughout the Midwest know, Allen is also the "antiques capital" of Michigan, and no self-respecting antiques hunter could ever blink and miss it without wondering just what they might have missed. Michigan Avenue is called Chicago Street in Allen, and the 1912 photograph above—featuring a horse-drawn wagon and a motorcar facing opposite directions in the center of the road—might be a fitting representation of how a small village has managed to balance the old with the new. Yet, despite the heavy stream of traffic that began running through Allen more than 100 years ago, the town still maintains its quiet side, much like the Edward Hopper–like feel of its post office shown in the 1919 photograph at right.

ALONG THE ROAD. Nothing better illustrates Allen's role as a stop along roadside America than the above photograph of Allen's Tourist Camp. Offering gasoline, automobile service, and tourist cabins, it would have been a welcome sight to travelers during the 1920s and 1930s. Allen is named for its first settler, Capt. Moses Allen, a veteran of the War of 1812. He and his family came to the area in 1827. The section of Chicago Street in the postcard below was taken in 1917. The message on the back is amazing in itself: "We have given up our play because one of the boys got shot. It did not kill him, but hit him in the ankle, and I guess it will probably cripple him. Yes, you want to try and come up to the dance, next Friday night!"

ANTIQUE ALLEN. Allen comes by its reputation as Michigan's antiques capital honestly. In fact, travelers along Michigan Avenue begin to encounter a seemingly endless line of small antiques shops, antiques malls, roadside stands, and seasonal flea markets long before entering Allen's city limits. For the seasoned, diehard antiquer, there are four large multi-dealer antiques malls located right in town. Perhaps the most memorable antique shopping experience can be found at Preston's Antique Gaslight Village, seen here. Located along Michigan Avenue, the Gaslight Village features several small antiques shops arranged in an outdoor village setting housed in more than 20 fully restored historic structures. (Author's collection.)

Chicago St. Looking West   Quincy, Mich.

QUINCY, MICHIGAN. When the first settlers arrived around 1830, the village of Quincy was considered part of Coldwater. The two villages separated in 1836, and the name Quincy was adopted at the suggestion of Dr. Hiram Allen, who had recently migrated from Quincy, Massachusetts. With a population of less than 2,000 residents, Quincy is considerably smaller than neighboring Coldwater, but its position along US-112 made for a thriving downtown business district. The road was known as Chicago Street in Quincy, and the photograph above provides a westward view, featuring the Quincy Hotel in the foreground. Like many small towns throughout America in the early years of the 20th century, Quincy was often host to travelling shows and circuses. In the undated photograph at left, Quincy residents are held spellbound by an acrobatic demonstration staged in the center of town.

THE PASSING SHOW. Above, in a rare photograph dating from the early 20th century, the Quincy Village Concert Band performs for local residents in the middle of Chicago Street. According to a note scrawled on the image's reverse, during the warmer months of the year the village band performed on this corner every week. The 1910 photograph below shows a family departing from the Quincy train station. Like many of the towns and villages along this stretch of the Chicago Road, Quincy was a major stop on the Lake Shore & Michigan Southern Railway line. Owned by the New York Central Railroad, the Lake Shore, as it was often called, was part of the company's main route between Buffalo, New York, and Chicago, Illinois.

NIGHT AND DAY. In the c. 1910 photograph above, Coldwater's Chicago Street (Michigan Avenue) is shown at night. In the early years of the 20th century, folks living in the "hinterlands" must have felt as though they had suddenly been vaulted into the modern age after seeing the main street of their hometown lined with and illuminated by electric lights. The dramatic impact of the innovation is evident, given the countless—and usually underexposed—photograph postcards that flooded the market at the time. Entitled, "Our Busy Day," the postcard below shows Coldwater by day. It was taken from a position very close to the image above, affording much the same viewpoint.

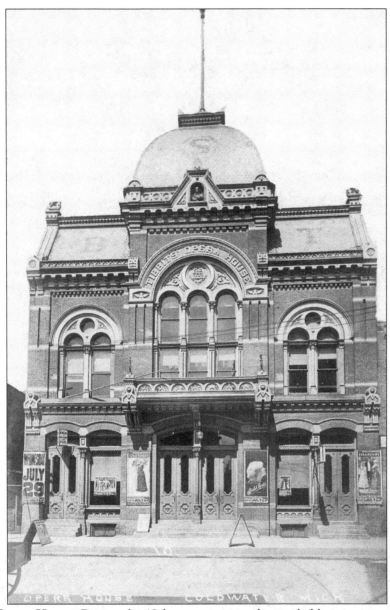

TIBBITS OPERA HOUSE. During the 19th century, opera houses held an important place in the social world of cities and towns throughout America. They were a sign of importance and prosperity and made it possible for communities to host traveling shows and lecture tours while providing a venue for local productions, social functions, and public presentations. In time, radio, motion pictures, and television made them obsolete, and most fell victim to neglect, eventually disappearing. Today, few of these opera houses still exist. Tibbits Opera House in Coldwater is one of the few, and perhaps greatest, examples still extant. Built in 1882 and funded by local businessman Barton S. Tibbits, the opera house cost an immense $25,000 and ultimately led to Tibbits's financial ruin. Ironically, it became his lasting gift. Over the years, Tibbits has hosted appearances by Buffalo Bill, Clarence Darrow, Thomas Keene, John Phillip Sousa, James Whitcomb Riley, and many more. Considered an architectural masterpiece, Tibbits Opera House is a priceless historic artifact still in use today.

WILLOW INN-LOG CABIN   FRED HURLEY, PROP
708 W. CHICAGO ST.   COLDWATER, MICH

WILLOW INN LOG CABIN. Dealing with the rustic accommodations associated with the stagecoach era might have been a little more enjoyable had they been a matter of choice. At Fred Hurley's Willow Inn Log Cabin, travelers could stop for a bite and briefly enjoy the illusion of dining in the "days of yore" knowing their car and the modern world awaited them just beyond the front door.

ARLINGTON HOTEL. While dining in a rustic setting might seem like an enjoyable novelty for some, sleeping in a rustic setting is a different story entirely. Coldwater's Arlington Hotel (far right) once offered some of the most prestigious overnight accommodations available along the route. Located at the corner of Chicago and South Hanchett Streets, the hotel was a familiar landmark to travelers for many years.

LOBBY, ARLINGTON HOTEL. This rare interior photograph of the lobby of Coldwater's Arlington Hotel looks like a scene from a late-1930s film. Summer sunlight illuminates the quiet, sleepy room as a man stands just behind the line of leather chairs with a folded newspaper in hand. The hotel clerk stands manning the check-in counter behind a glass showcase displaying a full line of cigars.

CLARKE. One of Coldwater's longest-running businesses was E.R. Clarke & Co., a druggist and grocer established in 1850. Clarke was devoted to the city, and in 1886 he financed the construction of the Coldwater Library building. The photograph shows Clarke's float for Coldwater's 1908 Fourth of July parade. With Clarke employees along for the ride, the float resembles a streetcar or trolley on the "Good Service Line."

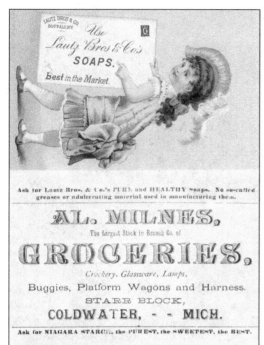

AL. MILNES. Another of Coldwater's long-term businesses was the Al. Milnes Store. Dominating the Starr Block along Chicago Street, Milnes was easily a one-stop shopping center of the past. The front of the two-sided 19th-century store card at left advertises Lautz Bros. soaps, and the reverse indicates that Milnes offered the largest stock of groceries in Branch County, as well as crockery, glassware, lamps, buggies, platform wagons, and harnesses. (Author's collection.)

CAPRI DRIVE-IN. Just west of Coldwater's downtown district, the Old Chicago Road runs past the playful neon and multi-bulb marquee of the Capri Drive-In. Opened in 1964, the Capri has been owned and operated by the same family for nearly 50 years. As one of Michigan's last surviving drive-in movie theaters, it is truly fitting that it is located along the state's oldest surviving highway. (Author's collection.)

BATAVIA AND BATAVIA CENTER. The area known as Batavia is located just west of Coldwater, with two villages sharing the name: Batavia, located along the Chicago Road, and Batavia Center, on M-86. The area was first settled in 1832 and named for Batavia, New York. It is still primarily an agricultural area, and residents of Batavia have long depended on nearby Coldwater for most of their business needs. While neither of the villages became thriving business centers, a post office was established in 1838, and there was once a station on the Lake Shore & Michigan Southern Railway line. The horse-shaped weather vane on top of T. Velie's Batavia livery stable (above) is the only evidence of the proprietor's line of business. In an undated photograph (below), several locals pose in front of the Batavia Creamery.

BRONSON. The city of Bronson is named for Branch County's first white settler, Jabez Bronson, who came to the region in 1827. Originally known as the village of York in Prairie River Township, both the village and the township were renamed Bronson in 1837. The 1913 photograph above shows the north side of Bronson's business district along with a muddy stretch of Michigan Avenue (called Chicago Street in Bronson). The image below, taken about 30 years later, shows both the north and south sections of Bronson's downtown business district. It also shows Chicago Street (US-112), a paved road by that time.

THE HORSE OPERA AND DOLLAR STORE. Clark's Opera House of Bronson was doing triple duty when the above shot was taken. While the text below the Cornice clearly declares the building to be Clark's Opera House, and there are several posters displayed about the walkway, the principal business seems to be the sale and servicing of carriages, harnesses, and bicycles. In the unusual photograph below, a couple stands amid its wares in what the caption notes as the "$ Saving Store—Bronson, Mich." Perhaps a forerunner of today's dollar store, it is doubtful that much of anything in stock sold for anywhere near a dollar given its vintage of about 1910.

THE AUTOMOBILE AGE. Above, an early Ford dealership is visible in the background of a tree-lined Chicago Street in downtown Bronson. In the foreground, another sign of the changing times brought on by the automobile age can be noted in the archaic and somewhat bizarre "Keep Right" sign in the center of the road. Consisting of a concrete pedestal with a vertical pole supporting a metal sign and topped with a huge red lightbulb, it is a fascinating anachronism of days long past. In the 1909 postal photograph card below, raised pedestrian crosswalks have been placed intermittently along the still-unpaved, muddy surface of downtown Bronson's Chicago Street.

WARM AND DRY. In a somewhat common theme found on Michigan postcards during the early 20th century, two "fishermen" pose above for a politically charged joke photograph. The inscription reads, "The Last Wet Day in Bronson, April 30, 1909," and in parentheses adds, "This is only water." The humor of the card comes from the fact that Bronson, and many towns and counties in the area, went dry in 1909—predating national Prohibition by several years. The photograph below shows the northeast corner of Matteson and East Chicago Streets around 1940. While the buildings in the image are still extant, the soda fountains are, sadly, long gone. On the corner at left is Hunsicker's department store with its front reading, "5 & 10" and "$1.00 & Up." Like the soda fountains, the local small-town department store is now a thing of the past.

STURGIS. Looking like a scene from the Old West, Chicago Street in the Sturgis of 1910, seen above, seems to be wholly dominated by the horse-and-buggy traffic. Despite the appearance, however, Sturgis proved to be one of the more progressive Michigan cities along the Old Chicago Road. Sturgis is the largest city in St. Joseph County, and its first settler was judge John Sturgis, who built a log cabin in the area in 1827. Originally known as Sherman and later as Ivanhoe, popular legend states that Gov. Lewis Cass suggested the name Sturgis in honor of the judge's wife because of his delight over the wheat biscuits she prepared for him during a dinner visit. True or not, the story makes for tasty folklore. The 1909 photograph below shows Sturgis from the west end of the business district.

INTO THE 20TH CENTURY. In the 1908 photograph above, the Sturgis Fire Department stands at the ready along Chicago Street. Though the automotive age was well underway, motorized fire trucks were not introduced until 1906, and the horse-drawn variety shown was still the most commonly used. In 1907, the City of Sturgis received $10,000 in funding for a Carnegie Library. In the photograph postcard below, crowds and carriages gather as residents of Sturgis witness the cornerstone-laying festivities at the corner of Chicago and Clay Streets. Funded through a program spearheaded by industrialist Andrew Carnegie, the Carnegie Library program granted matching funds to communities that qualified under the conditions of the program. To qualify, Sturgis had to demonstrate the need for a public library and provide a building site.

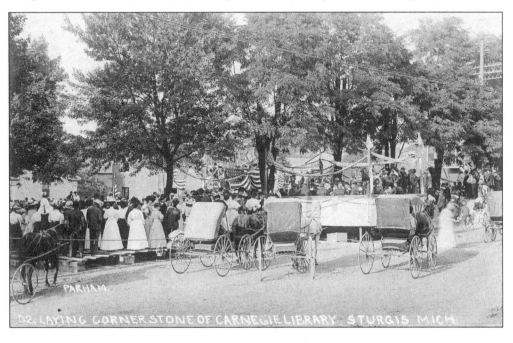

THE ELECTRIC CITY. By 1895, the electric age was sweeping the country, and while many larger cities had been wired for some time, folks in smaller towns were beginning to take interest in the advantages of electric power. In 1896, Sturgis built a coal-fired generator, making electric power available for three hours every evening. But the demand quickly exceeded availability. In 1911, the city took a daring leap forward, creating its own electric company and building a hydroelectric dam on the St. Joseph River. Sturgis celebrated the completion of the dam with a three-day event called Dam Days. In the photograph above, Chicago Street looks like a carnival midway as residents participate in the dam celebration. Below, one of the Michael brothers poses with his display windows after the family hardware store received first prize in a Dam Days display contest.

KLINGER, OR KLINGERS. Along the Old Chicago Road, west of Sturgis and just south of Klinger Lake, is an area once known as the village of Klinger (or Klingers on some maps). Originally settled in 1827 by Peter Klinger, the lake and nearby region is still predominantly agricultural and sparsely populated. In addition to the east-west traffic along US-112, the small village probably derived the bulk of its business from summertime vacationers seeking the quiet refuge of the lake. In the photograph above, Klinger Lake appears just beyond a small strip of homes and assorted buildings. Below, an undated image shows the interior of the Oakwood Pantry of Klinger Lake. Outfitted with a lunch counter (at right), the remainder of the establishment seems to be a grocery and general merchandise store.

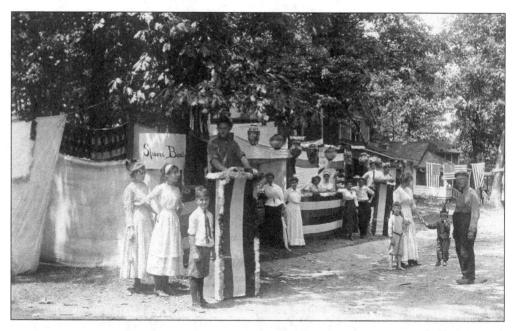

KLINGER LAKE REGION. Residents and summertime visitors pose for the undated photograph above while enjoying the festivities surrounding a patriotic holiday, most likely the Fourth of July. In 1878, records indicate the village and rail station were known as Douglas, and it was a stop along the Lake Shore & Michigan Southern Railroad. After receiving a post office in 1879, the small village was registered as Klinger's Lake, and the name of the depot was changed accordingly. The 1909 photograph below features the interior of the Davis Store of Klinger Lake. Heavily decorated with parasols suspended over tables and chairs, the airy, and seemingly sunny, hall most likely served as a summertime dining room.

INTERIOR OF DAVIS STORE. KLINGER LAKE, MICH.

OAKWOOD. The inclusion of Oakwood might qualify for a question mark; there seems to be little known about it. It once stood west of Klinger and is part of the Klinger Lake region, but there is almost nothing in surviving print referencing Oakwood as a place unto itself. The undated photograph above shows a young man resting on the porch of the Oakwood Tavern. An automobile stands idle beneath a windmill, and a half-obscured man stands in the darkened doorway. Though the structure is identified as the Oakwood Tavern, the photographer's inscription at the bottom identifies the scene as being in Klinger Lake. The skeletal framework of an unattended roller coaster seems almost eerie in the 1909 image below. Apparently part of an amusement park once located in the region, it is identified as Oakwood in the inscription at the bottom.

WAHBEMEME. The name Wahbememe may seem unfamiliar to many, as it is actually from the Native American Potawatomi language. In English, it means "white pigeon," and Chief White Pigeon was one of the Potawatomi's most famous chieftains. According to legend, in 1830 Wahbememe saved the white settlement at Millville by running more than 150 miles from Detroit to warn residents (who he considered friends) of an imminent attack by Native Americans during the Blackhawk War. While the chief succeeded in delivering his warning, he collapsed shortly thereafter, dying from heart failure. In honor of his friendship, heroics, and unselfish sacrifice, the village was renamed White Pigeon. The photograph above shows Chicago Street in White Pigeon in the early 1920s. Below, descendants of Chief Wahbememe (White Pigeon) gather near his honored grave, now a historic landmark in the village of White Pigeon.

THE REAL INDIANS: DESCENDANTS OF CHIEF WHITE PIGEON

CHIEF WHITE PIGEON. An "Indian" poses on horseback during a festival held in the early part of the 20th century. While the photograph is undated, it was likely taken during festivities held at the 1909 unveiling of the Chief White Pigeon Monument. While looking the part of the iconic Native American, the clothes worn by the individual are more closely associated with the American Plains Indians, not the Northeast Woodlands cultures prevalent in Michigan.

THE CIVIL WAR IN WHITE PIGEON. Cars, flags, and old soldiers line White Pigeon's Kalamazoo Street during a 1914 reunion of the 11th Regiment, Michigan Volunteer Infantry. Organized in White Pigeon in 1861, the volunteer force saw action in more than 15 major battles of the Civil War, including Chickamauga, Kennesaw Mountain, and the Siege of Atlanta. Overall, the unit suffered a casualty rate of more than 41 percent.

LAND GRANT OFFICE. White Pigeon is the oldest incorporated village in Michigan (1837) and holds an important place in the history of the Old Chicago Road. Still standing along White Pigeon's downtown business district is Michigan's oldest surviving US Land Grant Office. Operating from 1831 to 1834, the office once offered parcels of land at $1.25 per acre. It is now listed in the National and State Historic Registers. (Author's collection.)

TASTY NUT SHOP. A unique and tasty experience enjoyed by locals, as well as travelers along the Old Chicago Road, is White Pigeon's Tasty Nut Shop. The popular confectionary oasis has been in business since 1920, standing at the corner of Chicago and Kalamazoo Streets. Offering a wide variety of nuts roasted on-site, the shop also features a large selection of ice creams, sundaes, ice cream sodas, and fountain drinks. (Author's collection.)

Mottville, Michigan
Old Chicago c/b #3, built in 1867 by Joseph
Miller & Mahean Thompson. Torn down about 1927
by Roy Berger of White Pigeon, Alma Moore, Photo.

MOTTVILLE. At Mottville, the Old Chicago Road crosses the St. Joseph River. Settled in 1828, the small township and village is named for early settler Alva Mott. There have been several bridges built across the shallow stretch of the St. Joseph River in Mottville; the first two were constructed in 1833 and 1845. The rare photograph above shows a covered burr-arch truss bridge constructed in 1867. The covered bridge at Mottville was in service until 1927, when it was demolished. In the undated image below, a motorcar is seen rattling along the planks of the old covered bridge, while a horse-drawn wagon follows in the background.

THE BRIDGES OF MOTTVILLE TOWNSHIP. In the undated image above, the Old Sauk Trail approaches Mottville's covered bridge (1867–1927). By the early 1920s, as the old wooden bridge aged and travel along the highway increased, it became necessary to replace the structure. While not demolished until 1927, the covered Mottville Bridge was replaced in 1922 by the three-tiered (or spanned), concrete-reinforced bridge featured in the photograph below. Deriving its stylistic name of "camelback" from its hump-like design, Mottville's three-span, 270-foot bridge was used for automobile traffic until 1990. It is now preserved as a historic structure and used as a footbridge, standing alongside the bridge currently used to accommodate the heavy flow of modern-day traffic.

RUINS. Just east of the camelback bridge, an older pathway along the Old Sauk Trail leads to the banks of the St. Joseph River, where the covered bridge of 1867 once spanned. Here, ruins of the older bridge's abutments are still visible. Now overgrown with foliage and appearing as a series of tiny stone islands, they trace the old path that once forded the river.

DEER IN THE HEADLIGHTS. Old paint flakes from a sun-baked concrete deer sculpture as it sits tilted and forgotten along the Old Chicago Road. The abandoned motel in the background stands at a fork in the road, where US-12 (Michigan Avenue) turns briefly northward crossing the St. Joseph River and Michigan Highway 103 begins a short stretch before crossing into northern Indiana.

UNION AND ADAMSVILLE. As the road meanders westward from Mottville, it rolls through sparsely populated farmland, passing through the tiny villages of Union and Adamsville. Union dates from 1831, when Jonas Hartman opened a general store in the vicinity. The village center was moved to its current position alongside the Chicago Road in 1853. In the image above, Union School students pose with their teachers on March 12, 1909. Adamsville came about as the result of combining the smaller settlements of Adamsport, Christiana, and Sage's Mills. While they were all originally settled in the early 1830s, by 1838 they had been combined to create Adamsville. In the rare photograph below, the Adamsville Giants pose in a photograph dated July 4, 1910.

EDWARDSBURG. The small village of Edwardsburg was known briefly as Beardsley's Prairie, named after its first settler, Ezra Beardsley. In the space of a few short years, the name changed from Beardsley's Prairie to St. Joseph's, and finally Edwardsburgh in honor of the village's first merchant and postmaster. The spelling was revised to Edwardsburg in 1845. The photograph above shows the village post office and drug store, located on the northwest corner of Michigan Avenue at Cass Street. The same block is featured, from a slightly different angle, in the undated image below. While the crossroads pictured are still considered the center of the village, neither of these structures is still standing.

NILES. Michigan Avenue no longer runs through Niles, Michigan. Once a business route shared with Main Street in Niles, the road was rerouted during the early 1960s and now passes south of town. The photographs featured here were taken when US-12 (formerly US-112) passed through the city. The 1914 image above shows the old Main Street Bridge over the St. Joseph River in downtown Niles. Below, a photograph postcard dated 1912 shows a stately home on the tree-lined residential section of Niles's Main Street just before the road leads into the downtown business district. At the bottom, the card bears the inscription, "A Pretty View on Main Street, Niles, Mich."

FOUR FLAGS. The area now known as the city of Niles played an important role in history. Originally established by French Jesuits as a mission in 1690, it became a French military post known as Fort St. Joseph in 1697. The fort came into British hands in 1761, but it was captured by factions of the Potawatomi tribe in 1763 during Pontiac's Rebellion. Held briefly by Spanish forces in 1781, the fort was later abandoned, eventually becoming a part of the United States. As a result, Niles is known as the "City of Four Flags." There is little evidence of the city's military past in the 1906 photograph above, offering a view of Niles along Main Street during a busy day. Below, an undated image shows a different view of Main Street taken on a much quieter day.

THREE OAKS. According to local history, the village was settled by Henry Chamberlain in 1850 and named for a prominent cluster of three white oak trees. With that in mind, it may not come as much of a surprise to learn that most of the streets in Three Oaks are named for trees. Not even the Old Sauk Trail is exempt from the trend, as it runs through town under the assumed name of Ash Street. The main street in Three Oaks is Elm Street, and in the 1917 photograph above the bird's-eye view shows a southbound look at Elm Street running towards Ash. In the undated shot below, Elm Street appears in a northbound view. The unusual rounded roof of Drier's Meat Market is seen toward the middle of the street.

PRANCERS AND FEATHERS. Three Oaks is the setting for the 1989 film *Prancer*, and many exterior shots were filmed in town. In the photograph above, Elm Street is viewed from the Michigan Central (MCRR) tracks, which run through town en route to Chicago. In the image below, the Warren Featherbone Factory is seen midway down the street (right), a portion of its name visible on the wall. Three Oaks dry goods merchant Edward Warren founded the company in 1883 after discovering and patenting a method for using turkey quills to create a product that successfully replaced whalebone in the manufacture of ladies' corsets. As times changed, the company prospered, expanding its product lines to reflect emerging trends. In 1917, Warren founded the Warren Featherbone Foundation, a philanthropic organization that has donated property for parks and wilderness areas throughout Michigan.

NEW BUFFALO. When tooling along on US-12 westbound and counting down the last few miles toward New Buffalo, it is not unusual for travelers to sense they are coming to the sea. After the unlikely (yet, very real) experience of driving nearly 200 miles land-locked in the "Great Lakes State," it is refreshing to see the great expanse of Lake Michigan. Knowing that it is just up ahead, travelers might crane their necks as the road turns south, hoping to sneak a glimpse at the expansive water as they drive toward town. In the above photograph from the early 1920s, the golden age of automobile travel seems to be well underway as cars motor along US-12 in New Buffalo, Michigan. Below, downtown New Buffalo is seen from the corner of Whittaker Street and US-12.

LAKE MICHIGAN. This shot of an evening scene along the shore of Lake Michigan at New Buffalo dates from the late 1940s. The beach at New Buffalo is popular with vacationers from all around the southern stretches of Lake Michigan. Far from the urban shores of Chicago, and north of the industrial stretches of northern Indiana, New Buffalo's public beach seems removed from the working world.

"COOLEST SPOT ON THE HY-WAY." According to the back of a promotional card stating it is located "just one-half mile from the shores of Lake Michigan," New Buffalo's Hilltop Motel was one of many places available to vacationers drawn to the lakeshore. Showing a row of tourist cabins designed to resemble miniature castles, the motel's advertising card claims to be the "coolest spot on the Hy-Way" and sweetens the pot by offering television in each unit and a free television lounge. (Author's collection.)

Main St.
New Buffalo Mich.

MAIN STREET BY THE LAKE. In a photograph taken during the late 1920s, things seem to be heating up on a busy summer morning in New Buffalo. The buildings are already bathed in midmorning sunlight, and Lake Michigan awaits vacationers just beyond the scene. New Buffalo was originally settled in 1834 by Capt. Wessel Whitaker, who named the town in honor of his hometown of Buffalo, New York.

THE BURGER THAT MADE NEW BUFFALO FAMOUS. US-12 is Buffalo Street in New Buffalo, and coming into town along East Buffalo Street brings travelers face-to-face with Redamak's. Easily the most famous eatery in New Buffalo, Redamak's has been serving up its "world-famous hamburgers" since 1946. Open from March through October, Redamak's was purchased in 1975 by the Maroney family, who continue to keep the delicious lake-resort tradition alive.

Main Entrance to Hotel Golfmore, Grand Beach, Mich. 602

GRAND BEACH. From New Buffalo, it is a short distance down the Old Chicago Road to the Indiana state line. Along the way and just off the road, the shores of Lake Michigan have long been home to two popular resort villages: Grand Beach and Michiana. In the above photograph dating from the mid-1920s, the still-extant gates of Grand Beach welcome vacationers to the Hotel Golfmore (one can only imagine what went on there). Once a popular lakeside resort, the Hotel Golfmore, seen below, stands like a castle above the shores of Lake Michigan. While its opulent gates still welcome vacationers to the village of Grand Beach, the hotel was destroyed by fire in 1939. A popular vacation stop along the Michigan Central Railway, Grand Beach was founded in 1912 and has a permanent population of less than 200 residents.

Hotel Golfmore, Grand Beach, Mich.

MICHIANA. Lake Michigan is seen just beyond the beach in a photograph taken from the beach road at Michiana. The region known as Michiana runs along Lake Michigan from the extreme southwestern edge of Michigan into northern Indiana. It is a region of beaches and sand dunes. While the permanent population numbers less than 200, the area is very active with vacationers during the summer months. (Author's collection.)

Three

INDIANA, ILLINOIS, AND FORT DEARBORN IN CHICAGO

INDIANA. A small sign is all that indicates that US-12 has crossed the Indiana state line. From this point, the road winds a path through the western outskirts of Michigan City and then westward just south of the Indiana Dunes and the lakeshore. Unlike the trail through Michigan, the road in Indiana rarely crosses through the heart of the villages, towns, and cities along the way. (Author's collection.)

MICHIGAN CITY, INDIANA. As the Old Sauk Trail leads southward, it skirts past the Indiana section of Michiana and winds through the city limits of Michigan City past a handful of small motels, roadside stands, and filling stations. Settled in 1830 by Isaac Elston, Michigan City boasts a population of nearly 40,000. While most of Michigan City is unseen along US-12, the road does afford a view of the La Porte County Superior Courthouse (above) and the popular Blue Chip Casino (left). In the distance, the familiar site of a cooling tower serving a nearby coal-burning plant is often mistaken for a nuclear facility. Just a short drive from US-12, interested travelers can make a brief side trip to the Old Michigan City Light, one of the few lighthouses located in the state of Indiana. (Both author's collection.)

NATIONAL LAKESHORE. A black oak rises above the dunes. In addition to the state park, the Indiana Dunes National Lakeshore, established in 1966, encompasses more than 15,000 acres and includes many natural and historic points of interest. The Bailly-Chellberg Site includes a restored trading post that thrived in the area during the 1820s and the farmstead of Swedish immigrants dating from 1900. (Author's collection.)

BEVERLY SHORES STATION. The familiar sight of train stations serving the South Shore Line Railroad appears at intervals along the Dunes Highway. Each station is unique in design and architecture, often reflecting the personality of the community it serves. Pictured is the Beverly Shores Station. (Author's collection.)

WESTBOUND

TIME TABLES

SUMMER SCHEDULE
All trains operated on
CENTRAL DAYLIGHT TIME

Trains to
CHICAGO
(SIX CONVENIENT STATIONS)
KENSINGTON
63rd STREET
53rd STREET
ROOSEVELT ROAD
VAN BUREN ST.
RANDOLPH ST.
from
SOUTH BEND
MICHIGAN CITY
GARY . . EAST CHICAGO
HAMMOND
(and intermediate points)

Connecting Motor Coaches to
Michigan City
from
BENTON HARBOR
ST. JOSEPH
(and intermediate points)

Chicago South Shore and
South Bend Railroad

Schedule in effect May 13, 1946

SOUTH SHORE LINE. Since 1903, the South Shore Line Railroad has served northern Indiana with commuter train service from South Bend, Indiana, to downtown Chicago. Following the Old Sauk Trail in an almost completely parallel line through much of northern Indiana, motorists along the way remain in close sight of the tracks from the station at Beverly Shores, right through to Hammond, and on into Chicago's south side. This is a timetable for the South Shore Line from May 1946. Service to South Bend was expanded in 1992 to add a stop at the South Bend Airport. Currently, there are 20 stations served by the line. The electrically powered South Shore Line is one of America's few surviving interurban railroads. (Author's collection.)

THE RAILCATS. As the Dunes Highway rolls into Gary, Indiana, travelers encounter US Steel Yard, the stadium of Gary's South Shore RailCats. A professional baseball team and a regional favorite, the team is a member of the American Association of Independent Professional Baseball and has played in US Steel Yard since 2002. The team won league championships in 2005 and 2007. (Author's collection.)

ELGIN, JOLIET & EASTERN. Just across from the US Steel Yard is the only surviving steam locomotive of the Elgin, Joliet & Eastern Railroad (EJ&E). Built before 1920, the locomotive is a 2-8-2 Mikado. Sometimes referred to as the "Chicago Outer Belt Line" and the "J," the EJ&E is a rail line operating throughout the suburbs surrounding Chicago. (Author's collection.)

GARY LAND COMPANY BUILDING. In a city built quickly to meet the needs of a burgeoning steel industry, Gary's first permanent structure served many purposes. Now restored and standing across from Gary's city hall, the Gary Land Company building was erected in 1906, and over the years it has served as Gary's town hall, polling place, post office, and even high school. (Author's collection.)

GARY, INDIANA. In this image, Gary's city hall stands over US-12. The city hall is identical to the Lake County Superior Court building, and the two stand side-by-side. The city of Gary was founded in 1906 by the US Steel Company and named after the company founder, Elbert H. Gary (1846–1927). (Author's collection.)

376

29134 Michigan Avenue, North from Straus Tower, Chicago, Ill.

THE LOST TRAIL. From Gary, Indiana, US-12 plods along in a northwestern direction through East Chicago, Whiting, and Hammond, but it no longer closely follows the path of the Old Sauk Trail. Winding through the industrial-based urban communities, US-12 shares a designation with US-20 and US-41 and along the way is known as Industrial Highway, Cesar Chavez Memorial Highway, West Columbus Drive, Indianapolis Boulevard, and South Ewing Avenue. When it becomes East 95 Street, US-12 heads westward on its path across the continent. Historically, the Old Sauk Trail to Fort Dearborn becomes a bit obscured at this point, and it can be assumed that the trail stayed close to the western lakeshore, eventually merging with Chicago's Michigan Avenue. This stereoscopic view from the early 20th century shows Michigan Avenue approaching downtown Chicago from the south. (Author's collection.)

Monroe st. at Michigan ave.

MICHIGAN AVENUE AT MONROE STREET. Many years removed from the time of Fort Dearborn, the photograph above shows motorists and pedestrians crowding along the intersection of Michigan Avenue and Monroe Street in the mid-1920s. This is an interesting example of the importance of researching historical images. It was sold to David V. Tinder under the pretext of being an intersection in Detroit. Further research made it clear that it is actually in Chicago. While Detroit does have a Monroe Street, it does not intersect with Michigan Avenue. Below, a vintage photograph shows one of Chicago's most famous hotels. With original sections built in 1893, the Congress Hotel has been in business for well over 100 years and has accommodated eight US presidents. (Below, author's collection.)

Night in Chicago

MICHIGAN AVE. FROM LAKE FRONT
HOTEL CONGRESS

FORT DEARBORN DESTROYED-1858   THIS BUILDING IS ERECTED ON THE SITE OF FORT DEARBORN   OFFICE BUILDING ERECTED-1922

FORT DEARBORN. One of the chief destinations along the Old Sauk Trail was Fort Dearborn. Built in 1803 and named for Henry Dearborn (1759–1829), the fort once stood over the Chicago River at the modern-day intersection of Michigan Avenue and Wacker Drive. During the War of 1812, the fort was the site of a Potawatomi ambush known as the Fort Dearborn Massacre. Following the attack, the original fort was burned. A second Fort Dearborn was erected on the site in 1816 and served many military and non-military uses until it was destroyed by fire in 1857. The bronze relief above, created in the early 1920s, adorns the London Guarantee Building and is positioned so that it faces the river at the Fort Dearborn site. At right, a relief sculpture on the Michigan Avenue Bridge depicts the Fort Dearborn Massacre. (Both author's collection.)

WENDELLA BOAT TOUR. Just under the Michigan Avenue Bridge, the boats of the Wendella Sightseeing Company have become a familiar sight to residents and visitors alike. Founded in 1935, the city's original tour boat company provides a wide variety of tours and commuter services along the Chicago River and Lake Michigan. (Author's collection.)

CHICAGO'S WATER TOWER. A few short blocks north of the Fort Dearborn site is Chicago's water tower, one of the city's most familiar landmarks. Designed by William W. Boyington and built in 1869, the water tower was one of the few structures that survived the Great Chicago Fire of 1871. Today, it is the only surviving structure still standing. (Author's collection.)

The Paige Limousine on Michigan Avenue, Chicago

PAIGE
The Most Beautiful Car in America

THE New Paige enclosed models occupy an unchallenged position among the finest motor carriages of this country and Europe. In design and luxury of appointment they are unsurpassed by anything that the automobile market affords.

If you would be satisfied on this point, pay a visit to our dealer and let him show you the Sedan, Town Car, Limousine and Coupe. At the same time, you will learn of the three engineering features that insure perfect motor efficiency no matter how cold the weather may be.

PAIGE-DETROIT MOTOR CAR COMPANY, DETROIT, MICHIGAN

PAIGE. There is something about this 1918 advertisement for Paige Limousine that seems to tie together the route from Detroit to Chicago. Illustrated in a scene along Chicago's Michigan Avenue is a car manufactured in Detroit. Paige Automobile Company was founded in Detroit in 1908, and its first vehicle was called the Paige Detroit. The company was purchased by the Graham Brothers in 1927, and subsequent models became known as the Graham-Paige. Eventually, Graham-Paige moved much of its body-assembly operations to a plant along Michigan Avenue in Wayne, Michigan. In one further Michigan Avenue connection, in 1947 the Graham-Paige Company was absorbed by Kaiser-Frazier, which occupied the Willow Run plant as its chief production facility. (Author's collection.)

MICHIGAN AVENUE AT LAKESHORE DRIVE. Less than 15 city blocks north of the Fort Dearborn site, Michigan Avenue disappears into North Lake Shore Drive. It is the end of the route into Chicago, which began at Cadillac Square in Detroit. While the Old Sauk Trail continues westward, it does so from around the area of Ninety-fifth Street. Historians believe that when it joined the westbound trail from Fort Dearborn, the Native American trail followed a path that roughly paralleled Archer and Ogden Avenues. (Author's collection.)

DAVID V. TINDER. Born in Lima, Ohio, in 1926, David V. Tinder grew up in Flint, Michigan. During his working years, his interest in photographs and collecting became the focus of his free time. In the early 1960s, Tinder began collecting stereoscopic views. That interest soon grew to include all vintage photographs of Michigan, with a particular focus on Michigan photographers of the 19th and early 20th centuries. Today, the David V. Tinder Collection includes more than 100,000 photographic images. It is easily the largest and greatest collection of Michigan vintage and historic images in existence. This book could never have been completed without his incredible collection. Over the past years, Tinder's overall generosity and interest in sharing the collection has made it possible for many writers, researchers, and historians to utilize parts of it for many projects. In 2006 and 2007, his collection was featured in Michigan's Family Album, a major show at the Michigan Historical Museum. While Tinder is already in the process of donating the entire collection to the Clements Library at the University of Michigan in Ann Arbor, he is still providing access and materials to fellow researchers. He is currently finishing a directory of more than 8,500 early Michigan photographers. Thanks to Tinder, their images live on. (Photograph by Laura Freeman.)

BIBLIOGRAPHY

1928 Handy Railroad Atlas of the United States. Chicago: Rand McNally & Co., 1928.

Forster, Matt. *Backroads and Byways of Michigan.* Woodstock, VT: Countryman Press, 2009.

Hunter, Gerald S. *Haunted Michigan.* Chicago: Lake Claremont Press, 2000.

Romig, Walter L.H.D. *Michigan Place Names.* Detroit: Wayne State University Press, 1986.

Scott, Gene. *Detroit Beginnings: Early Villages and Old Neighborhoods.* Detroit: Detroit Retired City Employees Association, 2001.

Wilkins, Mike and Ken Smith and Doug Kirby with Jack Barth. *The New Roadside America.* New York: Simon & Schuster, 1992.

INDEX

Visit us at
arcadiapublishing.com

CPSIA information can be obtained
at www.ICGtesting.com
Printed in the USA
BVHW010957050819
555096BV00023B/1693/P

9 781531 651695